ANGLES OF REPOSE

CHRIS TUTTON

AVALANCHE  BOOKS

Published in Great Britain by Avalanche Books, England 2012

Printed by SRP, England

British Library Cataloguing in Publication Data. A catalogue record for this book is available from the British Library.

ISBN: 978-1-874392-60-6

By the same author:

Ariadne's Lament (1993)
Acnestis In Elysium (1995)
Ecumenical Shadows (1998)
Rain Angel (2003)
Seasons of Winter (2005)

Pendulum (2008)
Of Love and Hope (2010)
Seductive Harmonies (2012)

CONTENTS

THE CONSUMMATION OF BELIEF

We were tourists then. Sightseers. Back-
packing our spring kisses and trespassing
touches, caracoling in watery rhymes to find
the passing pearl of our seed. We were

wordless waders on amniotic streams,
embrionic amblers. Featherless dreamers beneath
treecreeping stars, pitchers of ripples,
continental catchers of sweet-scented smiles. We were

bleeding rivers of need into each other's unformed scars.
Becoming brittle in the strength of our union. Losing our
half drawn portraits amid the faceless blur of a
crowd of strangers. We were

destitute. Impoverished by baptismal immersion.
Owning nothing but our fear of loss.
Hawking our souvenir wounds for crumbs in
a thousand spectral countries of golden mists.

THE SNOW HAS PAINTED A FLOCK OF RED-WINGS ON THE TREETOPS

I sailed upon you,
a bouquet of
uncharted waters.

Gathered
the creels of
your love

from a
tangle of
mists. Fished on

the coral coasts of
your naked flesh.
Lived nameless

among the
street-beggars
of your heart

long after you
had crossed it.

SHORT CHAPTERS FROM SUNSET

Day kisses a rose onto twilight's face
from the blooming garden of its ember,
scenting darkening skin a sweet snare
for gullible drifters on the wing.

DARKNESS SHALL NOT LAY ITS BONEY FINGER UPON HER

She is an ageing woman now,
rich in tenderness and sorrow,
a cradle of motherless children,
a plume of delicacy. She glistens

iridescent, soft-lipped in mist-
lacy glades, in vernal frocks.
Courted by summer, she is
blossom; rosen-faced, forever

rising in the belly of a snakeskin sky
like a salver of tantalizing fruit
slithering golden from the cowled moon's
bandy-fingered snatch.

THE INSOLUBLE HARMONIES OF COLOUR

The old man sat down against a stump of reflection and began to strip the bark from his torment with a sharp intake of breath.
'I have,' he thought, 'always expected my dour palette to yield a colour bright enough to lead me, with no consideration of the canvas to which I may have applied it. My brushes were the rocks of my ignorance which I did not learn to use with delicacy, and my pigment I hid jealously beneath my contempt for the opinions of others. Now I am alone, and my paint has hardened beyond use.'
As he softly easeled his head on hands tangled like the knuckled roots of an ancient tree, he heard a chorus of sheep bleating a ruminating song while they ambled slowly towards him.
The old man recognised the song at once, and raised his gaze to meet the bearded face of a venerable bellwether.
'It's a simple song,' offered the bellwether as a greeting, with a smile. 'We chew, we sleep, we sing, we amble. The colours of our life are few and muted'.
'Yet you paint so beautifully with them,' replied the old man, moved and quieted by the unaffected honesty of the ram. 'I could not match your mastery.'
'We paint what we are able, old man, we make no study of our inability. Our song does not change with expectation.'
'Even so, do you never wish for more than you have?' asked the old man keenly, trying for a moment to comprehend the absence of desire.

13

'More suns? More grass? More sleep? More song? How would we profit from such a wish, or even the hope that such a wish may be granted?' shrugged the bellwether with a cordial chuckle.

'I have always wished for more,' sighed the old man apologetically, 'my life has been spent in the pursuit of a formula which would multiply my desires and secure my success. I realise now that my efforts have been wasted. I have not in all my searching found the words to my song.'

The bellwether looked thoughtfully at the old man and attempted to understand the nagging root of his anguish.

'We are sheep,' he began, following a few moments of puzzled headscratching and another good natured shrug, 'we have no comprehension of the meaning of your words.'

'My words are simple. I am a man, and as all men I burned with the desire to succeed. To be better than all other men, to confront my peers with my finery, to arm myself with riches, to cultivate envy among my fellows.'

'To what purpose?' begged the baffled ram.

The old man let loose a long sigh and looked hard into a hazy distance for a reply.

'To be accepted,' he mused at last, 'to be recognised as one of my flock. To follow what was expected of me. To be an example of conformity and to sing a song which everyone knew.'

'You are too clever for me, old man. We sheep are uncomplicated beasts; we greet the sun in the morning, meander over meadows in song, chew the sweet clover and frolic in silvery streams. If we were intelligent animals, maybe we too would cultivate desires and strive for success, but as it is, we can only marvel at the strange magic of your words and carry on

singing.'
And as the swelling sun shone like saffron on watery hills, the old man searched the stretched and pine-selvaged skyline for a cooling shower of unformed replies, while the bellwether ambled away with his bleating number toward a fresh green pasture, chewing and frolicking and singing the same song they had always sung.

THE GOSPEL OF DISAFFECTION

We knelt in supplication,
you and I, Godless;

orphaned by a
prevailing wind, we

became birds and
flew away into the

darkness of belief
that light had failed us.

REOPENING LINES

In that narrow egress
between the mire
and

the stained-glass sky,
the carrion and the
crow,

the hymn and the prayer,
we gradually became
the

fruiting notes of
nightjar's twilight
keening.

*   *   *   *   *

From the ice-floes of
apocalypse we
traipsed

bare and broken-footed,
to steal a march on
your

odious army and
plant a forest of
our

standards on the
summit of your
disapproval.

Glacial children,
refugees from your
frost

of fallen generations
slaughtered by
extrusion.

AN INESCAPABLE HORIZON

We skipped whole chapters to arrive here
thumbing the page of a new past
anticipating the key of our impending dirge
while listening to flowers
grow into summer evening breezes.

A DAY OF JUDGEMENT

The small boy offered his father a posy of beguiling
contemplations from an unfolding wasteland of opinions which
he had yet to successfully cultivate.
'Which should be my favourites, father?' he mused, excitedly
attempting to sniff out the subtleties of difference between them.
His father accepted the bouquet gently, and carefully arranged
the blooms of the small boy's discourse into a garbling babble of
bouncing balls with which the small boy immediately engaged,
talking hurriedly in reply to, and continuing to bounce as quickly
as he could. 'But how does this answer my question?' implored
the small boy after a short time, unable to contain his confusion
and already beginning to tire. 'I am no longer able to keep them
all bouncing, or even continue to hear what they are saying to
me. Could you not turn them into sand, so that I may lay easily
upon them and quietly enjoy the bed of them beneath me?'
His father raised a meditative eyebrow and lowered his gaze to
the confounded face of his faltering offspring.
'If you wish to rest easily on your contemplations, my son, your
favourites will be those which enable you to sleep. And if your
intention is to sleep comfortably on your bed of thoughts, your
contemplations will never be more than dreams.'

ANTIQUATED EPITAPH FOR THE BOY WHO UNWITTINGLY DRESSED EVERY- BODY ELSE IN IN THE PIECES OF HIMSELF HE THOUGHT HE HAD LOST

I watched you,
Fair of face
Misplace
Your only
Smile, as
You grew
Into dark clouds
Beneath Sunday's eyes.

YOUR UNBOWED
BEAUTY IS STILL
SOFT AS THE
LIFE OF A KISS

Such sweet breath
of love
remains

a willow-fleshed
fist of
gathered blooms.

Unspoiled. Tender
as suppliant lips
on the greening

cheeks of Spring. An
anchorage of sighs
where a

crowing billow of
circling
blackwings hurl.

THREE DEGREES OF SORROW HAD CAUSED THE BLOOD TO FREEZE IN HER VEINS

Little by little she lost
her voice in the wind.

She called and called
until all she could hear

was the night cracking
like a twig behind her.

YOU THOUGHT THAT IF YOU COULD CRUSH OUR HANDS WE WOULD NOT BE ABLE TO EMBRACE OUR PRINCIPLES

We were always more in our one
luminous voice

than you in your little puffyshirted
choir of contempt

however stealthily you tried to
take us from behind

we could always smell you coming.

LOVE LESSON

Love is
biting your
tongue when
another's tongue
has
bitten you.
Turning
another cheek
when
another's cheek
has
turned on you.
Love means
never having to
say you're
sorry;
because you've
already tried to
make it up
a thousand
times,
and you
know you
never will.

THE MATING RITUAL

He arranges colours
of expectant darkness.
In nine months
she will bear
him their open
wound of misfortune.

PATRICIDE: THE
CHILD DENIED

My father died
before I was born:

came home from
work every night

and grunted, like
we were to blame.

SOUNDTRACK FOR
THE ADVANCED
KARAOKE SINGER

There is a sound
like murderous
mothers
excusing themselves
to charred children.

Like words
hollered so loudly
they have fallen
shaken from the
shelter of their
meaning.

Like a caterwauling
choir of saintly
sacrifice
you were always
singing along to.

THE PAST HAS ARRIVED
TOO LATE FOR US TO
PROFIT FROM IT NOW
(GIVE ME BACK THE
HATRED YOU STOLE
FROM ME WHEN YOU
SANITIZED MY FEARS)

I need the rhythm of my anger to
Remember the words of my song,
And reassure my imperfections
That they were perfect all along.

THE RHYMER'S
DAYDREAM

There was no time to
stand and stare;
I didn't waste my life -
just forgot it was there.

IN FADING MEMORY OF THE MOMENT
WHEN WE COULD NAME EACH OTHER
WITHOUT PAUSING FOR REFLECTION

From that sickening shanty of
weatherbeaten words, to this
rain and ravaged harbour of embrace, we

tumbled abroad from the shadow of ourselves
like a wisp of fig leaves; frightened
fugitives in fingering woods.

From our weapons and our wales; our
epees of epigrams, foils of bitter phrases,
sabres of sarcasm sharper than any

tiger's tooth, and the appallingly naked
body of a time when we could still
fondly remember how we

sailed into each other
sea green and cuckoo'd
like a flotilla of suns.

THE CLOSING OF
SUMMER

Through the roundel the
wild goose steps out of

frame. Camera pans.
Anguish dresses the

stage in weeping ash.
Beneath a blind sun

The air is black with
the smoke of lovers.

OF ALL THE WONDERFUL WORDS IN THE WORLD, ALL YOU EVER LEARNED TO SAY WAS SORRY

This resplendent ship of sounds has sailed
to every blackened corner of the globe, with

colours of rainbow dreams splashed
blazing on its masthead. Has traded its

cargo of conjury to souls as lost as you, while
you grappled for a meaningful echo in its wake

on your little cobbled raft of contrition.

DON'T THROW YOUR BABY TO THE MOLOC, MOTHER DARLING

The child's need
for you,

a breasted
apex, a

towering love,
a thorny hug

beyond his
clutch

is written
indelibly

in an ink of
thumb-tacks

in the throat,
glass splinters

under the tongue,
vagabond words

bound into
skin covers

broken
spines

perpetual
bleeding.

ISLANDS

I lost my home when
my tears dried,
crusted into islands
I could never quite
sail away from.

SHORT CHAPTERS FROM
SUNSET: THE GARDENER

The tiller of the foundling tear
rakes the fallen leaves of his
child. Buries

his gathering storm in the
thrombotic glower of a
mereswine moon, as it keels

reeling beneath varicose
veils of mourning, and the
pitched breech of a

water-broken sky.

A STRANGE FOG IN
ENGLISH BAY
VANCOUVER 1981

The ocean swallowed her,
spat her out,

left her in ancient silence
on the ragged esplanade

of her undrowned sorrow.

THE APPRENTICE

Gradually she mastered
the language of old age;

the disaffected groan of
windshoved timber; the

victor's stooping lunge
to finish by a head.

THE LAP DOG

He was battle-scarred by compassion. Crippled by infinite
ascents. An anonymous shadow armed with the indignation of
his own inconsequence and a stiletto in his stare, he kept a
coffin-maker's count of casual casualties from killing fields on
which he had long since lost the stomach for a fight.
He could still kill all right; a litany of mutilated emotions lay
bleeding behind his black eyes to prove it. And innocuous
encounters were never innocent until proven guilty now.
He rode alone; on slaughterhouse streets of dissolution, beyond
the redemption of perspective, beyond the dereliction of
expectation and the necrotic dragnet of his implacable nemesis.
Once they were close as siblings, now he dreaded and detested
this filthy fallen bastard angel, mother-whore of the universal
death squad with the venom of a betrayed lover and confidante.
Now he could barely bring himself to spit its faecal name from
the buckled snarl of his speech-stained lips.
Ego; the misanthropic maniac; the psychopathic, cold blooded
trigger-finger of personality. The wormy little sense-eroding
bastard he had shared the choicest moments of his childhood
with - even entrusted his life to - was not only, he soon after
discovered at unfathomable cost, a weaselly, gut-rifling pilferer
who lifted his most treasured ideals and replaced them with a
worthless catalogue of cowardly compromises, but an assassin
with an oilslick of blood on its hands. And its bloody hands
were everywhere. Given half a glance they'd spill out of the jeer
of prying eyes like sniggering teardrops. Even names had finger-

prints on them. Faces and names were now summarily forgotten. Titles removed. Nomenclature ignored. The etiquette with which he had once excised the tumour of temptation to disembowel the living soul of an angel with a sneer eschewed. Now he would disembowel anything.

*   *   *   *

He grunted something indistinct to himself, as if someone could overhear the groan of his reluctant shuffle into daybreak.
He no longer sought sanctuary in the vacuum of semantics. Didn't trust words an inch. They had lost their power to heal. They had become murderous. They could seduce you into feelings. They could get you killed before you had time to throttle them. They were an abyss you could stumble into and drown. He'd never be such a fool to speak them again. Ever. Words could carry it concealed into the flab of your biddable brain by the back door. Decorate it in tongue-tinsel. Get it fat on the sound of itself. That was how you were forced to draw fast. That was how you were forced to justify raising your own little clutch of insidious and fatuous phrases that were only ever waiting to sentence you to your own fatal definition. To stand you against a wall of your own reckless ranting in a line of similarly unassuming idiots to be shot down for parting what was left of your teeth and letting the incriminating insignia all over the whole fetid uniform fall out. That was why the most reviled and stinking orifice had to be kept shut. Always. Anyway, besides the naked treachery of the thing, the abiding shudder of endlessly reliving the near-death experience of his mother forcing him to gulp down putrid gut-loads of her own

36

reeking pity like effluent at the dinner table of his infancy made
it almost insufferable now to have to prise the same execrable
hole open to stuff a fistful of food into it.
He was revulsed by the depravity of his childhood glut, almost
as much as he was sickened by the retch-making potbelly of his
gullible appetite.
He devoured his revulsion with the naked craving of a convert to
an incomprehensible cause, and with a vomit-hued abstract
expressionist palette of supercilious self loathing, imagined
himself as a lap dog on the turn with an insatiable hankering for
a mouthful of really good groin.

*   *   *   *

Morning dripped semen-like out of glandpurple wings on cue
and addressed the new day in cliches, laughing at its own joke
over and over again. It yapped a shrill, ill-defined invitation
incessantly like some witless trouper's hackneyed catchphrase,
before unceremoniously hammering the tenon of its echo into
the cheap-scented, open-thighed mortice of another
streetwalking afternoon.
A light wind blew bits of its own story around lengthening
shadowed sidestreets like a weekend wedding. Splinters of
conversation followed entangled shapes like bridesmaids. In the
sabre-rattling semi-distance identities were brokered in shops
and offices. Personalities were midwived by illuminations. Post
natal blood trickled into gutters.
He patrolled the perimeter of his internment with an affected
limp, alternating the broken glass bead between diced heels,
affording himself the almost decadent luxury of a genuine

37

bespoke grimace to conceal the underbelly of expressions he could no longer risk in public. There were perverts everywhere. Beneath cherry trees shingle bearded the manicured park which drew up quietly alongside his hobbling amble. The pond spilled out into a sort of silvery sewer where ducks floated about like refuse. He almost smiled. Somewhere he could hear small, sharp, throat-stuck bones of skeletal songs. The sudden screech of black ducks turning on brown ducks yelled back in cacophonous counterpoint. More disturbingly, ego had been roused, and was crawling out of the slime.

*   *   *   *

In the self-harmed evening's open scar machinations merged and festered sickening beneath the weeping fixed ulcerated eye of a January moon. Open-overcoated winos teetered precariously like broken-winged crows silhouetted against the darkening contours of resilient memories. Streets with hidden hills became shouting galleries aflame with the scorching, naked volume of punctuated personality. An arsenal of weaponry was conceived in spontaneously contrived poses. He took cover. Crossing the road into a more comfortable submission, he made his way home through a minefield of glances.

*   *   *   *

He ran his finger over the indented line which ran like a camp track across the hard, powdery sheen of her little pink circle. She looked pretty in pink. It was just the right shade for her. Whispering obscenities, and sucking his fingers as he brushed them lightly over her face, she taunted him playfully with her flesh. He was drooling. He had never been this close to a real woman. He kissed her slowly, licking her lips, drinking her bitter spit. Kissed her again and again, rolling her forked tongue in his mouth, tasting her putrid personality on the back of his throat, swallowing the crumbling venom of her promise. They kissed and kissed, sucked and sucked, until both were so dry they could no longer swallow.

By the ice cold coloratura chorus of dawn they had already been laying still on the overstretched catafalque carapace of night belly to belly for hours.

ON THE BENT KNEED BROKEN IOPTEROUS DAWN I PLUNGED WITH A RELUCTANT SYMPHONY OF OUTSTRETCHED ARMS FLAPPING AND WAVING FROM THE PRECARIOUS LEDGE OF DREAMS TO THE DUBIOUS INFIRMARY OF YOUR NETTLED CARESS

Night died in suspicious circumstances.
The casualty lay between yes and no
in a wilderness which would not yield
to reason.
We carried the body home and bathed it
in puerile reassurances about
severed veins of trust.
Without that familiar darkness
we were never likely to sleep for long.

THE TRANSPOSITION
OF DESIRE

I miss the play of your light
upon my shadow and stone
where I dream undiscovered
apostrophes.
I miss your tender hedgerows
gathering lustrous threads of
morning silk you
braided for drawstrings of
our twilight's skyline.

PAINTING WILTSHIRE BY SEASONS IN
A REALISTIC RANGE OF SOFT COLOURS
AND UNEXPECTED RHYMES

Sabled painters spread spring canvases over
Heytesbury hills,
Sap green on titanium white;
Pointillist.

Crocus easels the thaw,
Offers up the thumb,
Slides across the
Sludge-grey ochre weave, wet on wet.

Sherrington summer sun drips like Pollock
Painting gold on the glass of Wiltshire water,
Lapwings bristle-stroke Crockerton skies seeping
Toward the gilt frame edge of Shear.

Bidcombe nestles in autumn rust, bleeds
Leaves against October's thrust; sows sepia sprigs in
Scribbler's eyes, before winter glazes ground a frosty
Palette of sighs, wind on bough, naked

Shrubbery shrill, tears pigment from
Codford and the Deverills; smudges on the
Fingerprint of another year, then draws
Night impasto over its own signature.

...AND THE BASILISK SHALL SPRING FROM THE SEED OF THE SERPENT

Unsceptred he straddles
the reign of his plaint,

bending
bitter as prayer
at the knee.

Glutting on the
birthblood of
his eventual breath,

the tree of life is heavy
with the blossom of death.

A BAPTISMAL DROWNING. PART 1: THE IMPENDING IMMERSION

Matilda pulls me closer to water;
little hand
still wet with rain.

HIPPOPOTOMONSTROS-
ESQUIPPEDALIOPHOBIA

'I have tied myself in knots
with words',
sighed Martha,
trying to free herself
from an endless maze of
misinterpretation.

SAY YES TO HAPPINESS

'I'd say yes to happiness,'
thought Nigel,
staring through the steel fog of
a barbiturate sunset,
'if I wasn't always just
too damned depressed to
communicate with it.'

DEMENTIA

Icarus marched homeward,
circling his hospital bed

like a kite;
'I have fallen from the sun,'
he thought,

suddenly noticing that
everything felt colder.

AN INDOMITABLE
HUNGER

We would famish
before we

feed each other
crumbs from

this skin we
dare not call our own.

ANGLE OF REPOSE

The old man hung a limp arm
around the shoulder of his solitude and
married a melting wince to the moon.
'Another day has flown my nest,' he sighed,
plucking childhood souvenirs
from quiet nurseries of nightfall.

BRIDES OF TWILIGHT

We were brides of twilight
wedded to a sombre sun,
falling into darkness
like a confetti of stars.

A PASSAGE OF INGRESS

We set our little boats on the
drift of this endless turning of
tides. Now

waving, now touching, now
tumbling on the awkward
sands of

each other; beaches which
tomorrow will be peopled by
strangers.

THE CONSECRATION OF STONE

You raise me, a feather on your wing,
to the briny brim of my meltwater;

submerge me in the pacific current of
your parting lips; flow into me, a

tributary of transfiguration;
lead me like a dove to the

baptismal flood of your kiss.

CONSORT OF SHADOWS

The first frosts have harvested
a church of tender flowers; the

skylark scrawls. Wet evening
bell pulses through dry veins

of turned leaves and promises
to spend and save each dowry,

every burnished copper penny,
this alimony of autumn days.

48

THE EYE OF THE STORM IS
FULL OF TEARS

Between the sweet notes of this
blackbird's song lay the ghosts

of ramblers, who embarked upon

endless excursions into canyons
of darkness, who trampled thorns

of apprehension, who screamed

halfway around a world of voices
to return as a moment of silence.

THE BIRTH OF REBIRTH

I have arrived again
at the point of
my departure,

like an eternal chrysalis
always

attempting to escape
the skin of
my cocoon.

THE BECKONING

You invite me to the
easy arena of your
toppling eyelids.

Clench a shallow
breath to your chest.

Your smile lingers;
an uncertain child,

then wavers like the
fingers of a cornfield.

YOU OFFERED ME YOUR LOVE AS AN IMPOSSIBLE BARTER. I ACCEPTED IT AS A MORSEL TOO DELICATE TO SKEWER WITH A PITCHFORK

When it became impossible to converse,
we addressed each other with

euphemistic glances; each of us
unsure of the price

of dropping our gaze.

STUPIDITY IS THE
WORK OF IDIOTS

'I'd like to think of myself,'
sighed Nigel, trying to fit
a square aphorism into a
round whole,
'as the thinking man's
lapse in concentration.'

STILL LIFE
WITH
GOLDENROD
AND
NIGHTSHADE

The soulless
sentence of
your kiss was
never more
than skin.
Artless words
which could
not bridge the
distance of
their meaning.

A DECORATIVE DISCOURSE

For a peppercorn rent we

                      continued to occupy those

little spaces between us where

                      the furniture of our differences had

become painfully comfortable.

THE INEVITABLE CATASTROPHE OF INTERPRET-
ATION BEGETS THE UNNATURAL BASTARD BIRTH
OF DISILLUSION

Wounded in crossfire reverie as the sun fell masquerading as
                                                 sleep.
Waking faithparched, shaken, breathless, to discover the
                                    bleating dreaming blind.
Invoking reassurance from solemn psalms of abbreviated
                                               glances,
Crouching in such shallow phrases our thoughts could not
Pose naked for the night.

Threading ritual-sophist spangle onto starsplit drapery of
                                         deception
Frostwoodsandled, scalpel cold. Bluff-carved hunkering anxious
                                         beneath a
Cherry minted thirty pieces of browblood burnished silver moon
                                         swollen
Easeled between quivering aleamber thighs of impenetrable
                                             scars,
Painting the stray lambs of our whimpering shadows newborn
                                           soft,
Unkilned still by regret, cadaverous stains of arpeggiated
                                         evening pallor.

VERNAL ODE

Oh spring,
Sweet scent of

Putrifying winter,

I lie enraptured on
Your bed of bulbs

Like a leper

Ravished by
A nun.

YOU WERE THE PICTURE ON THE WALL OF MY SOUL

A PRETERNATURALLY SANCTIFIED SUPERMODEL CENTREFOLD

AN ETHICAL ICON WHO WAITED UNTIL I WAS BORN TO ABORT ME

You were old enough to be my mother,
mother. To carry the cross of your halo. To
cling by both nipples to your crown of thorns.

You were artful in your passion to define us,
divide us, determine the fighting weight of
our scrap. To deck me in the opener. Snip

greedily away below my belt. Me, the broken
egg, the fetid yolk of your youth. You, the
insatiable quaffer of the holy bilge. The

smoker of God's reefer. You, the beatified
pythoness, divining your martyrdom from the
scaffold of your sacrifice. Me, the invincible

inchworm gasping on your unfiltered umbilical
roach, drunkenly trashing the cheap furnishings
of my hotel womb.

THERE WERE DAYS WHEN I COULD NOT FIND YOU ANY-WHERE IN YOUR PORTRAIT OF CLOUD

and then there were days when you
landed me lazily with invitations to

gasp speared like a half-baked sprat on
the smoky spit of your amber eye, set

soft and dewy jewelled in the unleavened crown
of your fathomless dark and wheedling sea.

ANOTHER BEAU TO YOUR STRING

Ah, how you reeled him in, dripping with
morning, green and lush. How you stole

him from his fields of corn, plucked hollow
the orchard of his eyes. Fed him to the

famished cane of your command. Lost him in
your ramshackle coterie of tumbledown days.

WHEN LOVE WAS GOLDEN

When you were unable to fly
I carried you inside my shirt
like a prayer. Took you to

the tops of the beeches,
fledged you with little
nudges of trust. Kept you

on the gilt pages of my
day, read you
until the snows came.

THE TOUCH

We became
above
the axis of
flesh
beneath lilac and rain
in silken arcs of sighs
a touch
the endless orbit of
a kiss.

THE ASYLUM OF VENUS

I found you roosting beneath the
rafters of my wandering, nesting

amid the aching branches of my
interminable embrace; my kisses

carrying you softly as the wind,
without even stirring your curls.

YEARNING A LIVING

I collected you from
fountains

I threw myself into
bit by bit,

spending you on
little luxuries

I could have never
otherwise indulged.

THE SUTURE OF DREAMS

We thread summer through
the eye of a

needle, thimble up the knee,
stitch our little

shivers to these
sackcloth weeds of winter.

SOMEBODY SOMEWHERE
IS DYING TO BE BORN

Bring on your muscle of morning,
pit your risible fist against mine;

I stared down the night I was
afraid of,

and it was darker than you.